BUGGED OUT!
The World's Most Dangerous Bugs

KILLER
KISSING
BUGS

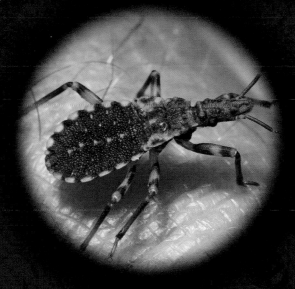

by Kevin Blake

Consultant: Paula L. Marcet, PhD
Research Biologist
Atlanta, Georgia

BEARPORT
PUBLISHING

New York, New York

Credits

Cover, © Nature Picture Library/Alamy; TOC, © Schlyx/Shutterstock; 4L, © Mihtiander/iStock; 4R, © Karolina Paniagua; 5, © Nature's Images/Science Source; 6L, © Karolina Paniagua; 6R, © Rattiya Thongdumhyu/Shutterstock; 7, © David Mercato/Reuters/Newscom; 8T, © Etotalora/CC BY-SA 4.0; 8B, © Rachael Curtis-Robles; 9, © Eye of Science/Science Source; 10T, © WHO/TDR; 10B, Public Domain; 11, © Nature Picture Library/Alamy; 13T, © Stringer/Argentina/Reuters/Newscom; 13B, © Tomas Bravo/ Reuters/Newscom; 14, © Smiley Pool/Belo Media; 15T, © scyther5/iStock; 15B, © Tomas Bravo/Reuters/ Newscom; 16, © John Cancalosi/Alamy and © Rtstudio/Shutterstock; 17T, © Stephen A. Klotz; 17B, © Nigel Cattlin/Minden; 18, © Smiley Pool/Belo Media; 19T, © Syda Productions/Shutterstock; 19B, © xraysonline/ CC BY-SA 4.0; 20, © Edgard Garrido/Newscom; 21, © STR/Reuters/Newscom; 22TL, © Gado Images/ Alamy; 22TR, © Gado Images/Alamy; 22BL, © Vanessa Becker-Miller/Shutterstock; 22BR, © Jaco Visser/ Shutterstock.

Publisher: Kenn Goin
Senior Editor: Joyce Tavolacci
Creative Director: Spencer Brinker
Photo Researcher: Thomas Persano

Library of Congress Cataloging-in-Publication Data

Names: Blake, Kevin, 1978– author.
Title: Killer kissing bugs / by Kevin Blake.
Description: New York, New York : Bearport Publishing, [2019] | Series:
    Bugged out! the world's most dangerous bugs |
    Includes bibliographical references and index.
Identifiers: LCCN 2018047309 (print) | LCCN 2018051909 (ebook) |
ISBN 9781642802399 (ebook) | ISBN 9781642801705 (library)
Subjects: LCSH: Conenoses as carriers of disease—Juvenile literature. |
    Conenoses—Juvenile literature.
Classification: LCC RA641.C66 (ebook) | LCC RA641.C66 B53 2019 (print) |
DDC 614.4/3—dc23
LC record available at https://lccn.loc.gov/2018047309

For more information, write to Bearport Publishing Company, Inc., 45 West 21st Street, Suite 3B, New York, New York 10010. Printed in the United States of America.

10 9 8 7 6 5 4 3 2 1

Contents

A Silent Kiss

In 2015 in Costa Rica, Karolina Paniagua came down with a high fever and **joint** pain. Over the next couple of weeks, she felt much worse. "I got to a point where I did not have strength in my legs. I could not walk," Karolina remembered. No one could figure out what was wrong with her.

A beach in Costa Rica

Karolina Paniagua is from Costa Rica, a small country in Central America.

Even after Karolina went to the hospital, doctors couldn't find the cause of her alarming **symptoms**. When the mystery disease began attacking Karolina's heart, the doctors knew they had to take action to save her life. One doctor decided to test Karolina's blood for Chagas (SHAH-guhs) disease—a deadly illness spread by kissing bugs.

Some kissing bugs carry tiny **parasites** that cause Chagas disease.

A kissing bug, which is also called a triatomine

5

Difficult Treatment

When the doctor told Karolina that she had Chagas disease, she was shocked. Karolina had no memory of getting bitten by a kissing bug. Doctors immediately gave her a drug to kill the parasites in her body. The treatment, however, made her feel even sicker. "I spent the time throwing up," Karolina said. Eventually, she began to recover.

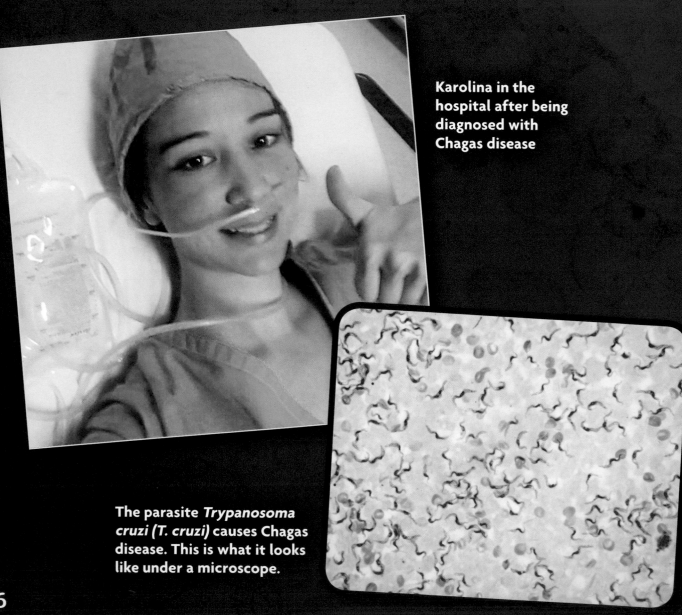

Karolina in the hospital after being diagnosed with Chagas disease

The parasite *Trypanosoma cruzi (T. cruzi)* causes Chagas disease. This is what it looks like under a microscope.

However, Karolina learned that even with treatment, she might not be **cured** of Chagas disease. The parasites can live inside **victims** for decades. "I know the symptoms will probably return," worries Karolina. All she can do is hope the disease will not get worse.

About six to seven million people, mostly in South America, are **infected** with the parasite that causes Chagas disease. About 12,000 people die from the disease each year. Most did not know that they had the disease.

A man gets tested for Chagas disease in Bolivia, in South America.

Hide and Suck

As Karolina learned, the kissing bug is anything but sweet. During the day, this **nocturnal** insect hides in walls or **crevices**. It also rests in piles of wood and birds' or other nests. Once it's dark and cool outside, the pear-shaped insect comes out from its hiding place to seek blood. It often enters people's living spaces to feed.

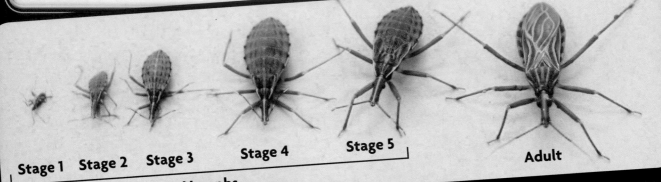

Stage 1   Stage 2   Stage 3   Stage 4   Stage 5   Adult

Nymphs

Triatomine bugs start out as eggs, then become nymphs, and finally grow into adults. As adults, kissing bugs have wings and can live up to 24 months.

Kissing bugs are about 1 inch (2.5 cm) long. There are over 100 different kinds. Almost all feed on blood.

Triatomines were given the name "kissing bugs" because they tend to bite on or near a person's mouth, where the **tissue** is soft.

While a person is asleep, the kissing bug often crawls onto the lips. Odors and heat help guide the bug to the victim's mouth. Then the insect stabs its needle-like mouthparts into the person's skin and sucks blood. It feeds until its body grows to the size of a grape. Once full, the bug then defecates—or poops—close to or on the bite!

A kissing bug's needle-like mouthpart is called a proboscis (pruh-BOS-kis).

Also known as the vampire bug, a kissing bug can feed for as long as 25 minutes. Most victims do not feel the bug sucking their blood.

Two Phases

The kissing bug's poop may contain the parasite *Trypanosoma cruzi*. If a person accidentally rubs the waste into the bug bite **wound** or touches his or her mouth or eyes, he or she can become infected. "Once the parasite enters your body, it's able to **hijack** cells," says Rosa Maldonado, a professor and researcher in Texas.

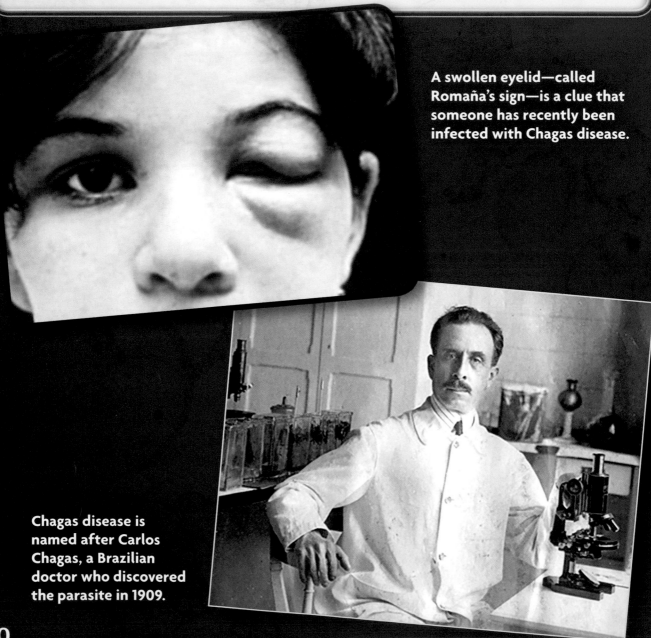

A swollen eyelid—called Romaña's sign—is a clue that someone has recently been infected with Chagas disease.

Chagas disease is named after Carlos Chagas, a Brazilian doctor who discovered the parasite in 1909.

During the first, or acute, phase of the disease, victims can experience fever, vomiting, headache, and a rash. While these symptoms often go away quickly, the parasites may remain inside the body for years. During the second, **chronic** part of the illness, the parasites attack a person's **organs**. They can seriously damage the heart, brain, and intestines—leading to death.

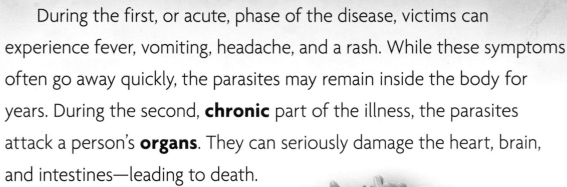

If given early enough, medicine may destroy the parasites. During the chronic phase, however, there is no cure for Chagas disease.

Not all kissing bugs transmit Chagas disease. The insects only carry the dangerous parasite if they've sucked blood from an infected person or animal.

Spreading North?

Kissing bugs are most common in Central America and South America. They also live in southern parts of the United States. However, some may be spreading farther north. Why? As **climate change** warms the planet, kissing bugs are now able to survive in places once too cold for them.

Kissing Bug Distribution in the United States

Reported
Potential

About 300,000 people in the United States have Chagas disease. Many were infected with the disease in Central America or South America before moving to the United States.

"As we get warmer climates . . . we may see more of certain kinds of infections," explained Dr. William Schaffner, an expert on infectious diseases. Doctors in Texas and other warm southwestern states are now on the lookout for this horrible illness. The Centers for Disease Control and Prevention (CDC) estimates that there are 37,000 people in Texas living with this parasitic infection. Many have no idea that they have the disease.

The flimsy walls of this building are a great place for kissing bugs to hide.

A woman gets tested for Chagas disease.

Infected!

Unfortunately, some Americans first learn about Chagas disease when they hear they are infected. That's what happened to Candace Stark of LaGrange, Texas. After she **donated** blood, Candace received a letter that said she had Chagas. "I was frightened of what was going to happen to me," Candace said. "I didn't know if it was going to kill me at the time because everything I'd read was terrible."

Doctors confirmed that at least twenty people **contracted** Chagas disease in Texas in 2016. There may be many more who simply don't know they now carry the parasite.

"If I could make a living walking around telling people about this disease and my experience, would I? Yeah, I would," said Candace Stark, who's pictured above.

Candace doesn't know how she got Chagas disease. Thankfully, she hasn't had any symptoms. Doctors gave Candace medicine to fight the parasites, and now she just hopes for the best. "I don't know if [the drug] worked," she worries.

During the chronic phase of Chagas, medications won't cure the disease. They may help slow its progression, however.

People can also get Chagas disease from infected blood. In addition, mothers can pass the disease to their unborn babies.

Bad Bites

While Candace Stark didn't know if she had been bitten by a kissing bug, Jennifer Bankston knew right away. One day when she was sitting on a wood deck outside her parents' house in Mason, Texas, she felt something extremely itchy on her legs. When Jennifer looked down, she saw several bites from kissing bugs! "I have had **severe** itching on every place I was bit," Jennifer complained. Then she noticed a few bugs between the cracks of the deck boards.

Kissing bugs often live in old wood.

Over the next few days, an **allergic** reaction caused the bites to swell and turn red. Doctors gave Jennifer a shot to reduce the **inflammation** and also tested her for Chagas. Fortunately, the bugs didn't pass along the disease. "People need to get rid of those bugs," Jennifer said. "They may be called kissing bugs, but they are dangerous."

A bite from a kissing bug

Some people are so allergic to kissing bugs that they can have difficulty breathing after a bite.

A kissing bug filled with blood. The insects can consume four to eight times their body weight in blood!

Pets at Risk

Kissing bugs don't just make people sick. They also affect pets. Kiska, a Japanese spitz dog, loves catching and playing with bugs near her home in Plano, Texas. One day, she carried a kissing bug into the house. Her owners saw the strange bug and tried to grab it. As they did, Kiska playfully **lunged** at it and gobbled it up.

Kiska, with one of her owners

The next week Kiska began having a heart attack every fifteen minutes! She was rushed to the **veterinarian** to try to save her life. The fluffy white dog underwent emergency **surgery**. Doctors gave her a **pacemaker**, which kept Kiska's heart beating. Without it, she would have died from Chagas disease.

Many dogs in the United States are affected by Chagas disease.

Chagas disease can cause a lot of damage to a dog's heart tissue and eventually lead to heart failure and death.

A pacemaker in a dog

Bug Hunters

Scientists are developing new ways to combat bloodsucking kissing bugs and Chagas disease. "The more we investigate, the more we will find," said Dr. Sheba Meymandi, a Chagas disease researcher.

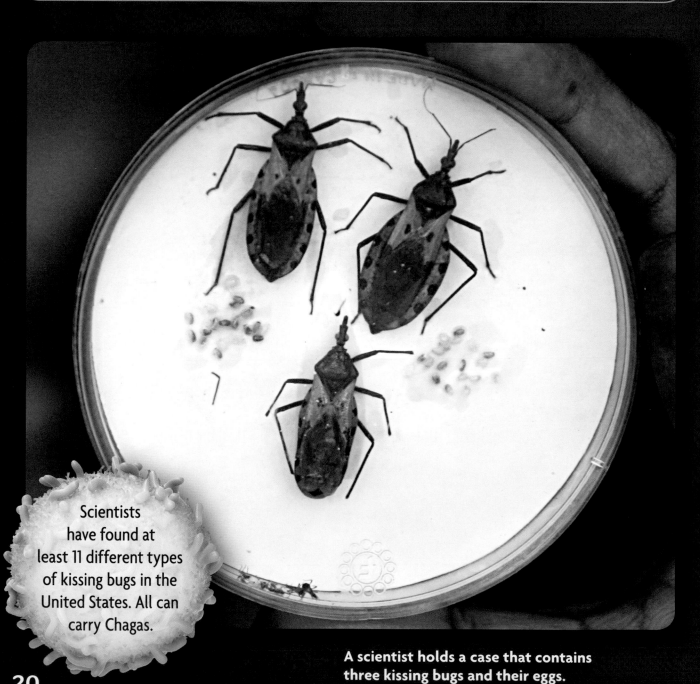

Scientists have found at least 11 different types of kissing bugs in the United States. All can carry Chagas.

A scientist holds a case that contains three kissing bugs and their eggs.

Scientists at Texas A&M University have asked ordinary people to catch kissing bugs and mail them to a **laboratory**. There, researchers can study the insects and test them for *T. cruzi* parasites. Plus, collecting the bugs can help spread the word about the dangers of the disease. According to one scientist, "It engages people and increases awareness of the risks."

Many Texans are happy to lend a hand in the fight against kissing bugs.

Related Diseases

Chagas disease and African trypanosomiasis (trih-pan-uh-soh-MAHY-uh-sis), also known as sleeping sickness, are caused by closely related parasites. This chart compares the two diseases.

	CHAGAS DISEASE	AFRICAN SLEEPING SICKNESS
Which Parasite Causes It?	*Trypanosoma cruzi*	*Trypanosoma brucei*
Which Insects Spread It?	Kissing bugs—brown or black-and-orange insects that live in the Americas	Tsetse (TSET-see) flies—small gray-brown insects that live in Africa
What Are the Symptoms?	First Phase: Fever, eyelid swelling, headache, and nausea Second Phase: Damage to the heart, brain, and intestines, which can lead to death	First Phase: Fever, headaches, joint pain, and itching Second Phase: Difficulty sleeping, confusion, **paralysis**, and death
How to Prevent It:	Seal up cracks around windows, walls, roofs, and doors. Remove wood piles near your home.	Wear long shirts and pants and insect repellent. Avoid blue clothing because the color blue attracts these flies.

Glossary

allergic (uh-LUR-jik) caused by an allergy, or physical reaction to something in the environment that's harmless to most people

chronic (KRON-ik) long-lasting

climate change (KLYE-mit CHAYNJ) the warming of Earth due to environmental changes, such as a buildup of greenhouse gases that trap the sun's heat

contracted (kon-TRAKT-id) got a disease

crevices (KREV-is-iz) small, narrow openings

cured (KURED) to be disease free

donated (DOH-nayt-id) to have given without recieving payment

hijack (HYE-jak) to take over

infected (in-FEK-tid) affected with a disease

inflammation (in-FLUH-may-shuhn) when part of the body becomes red, swollen, and painful due to infection or injury

joint (JOYNT) a place in the body where two bones meet

laboratory (LAB-ruh-tor-ee) a place used by scientists to conduct experiments

lunged (LUHNJD) moved forward quickly and without warning

nocturnal (nok-TUR-nuhl) active mainly at night

organs (OR-guhnz) parts of the body, such as the heart and liver, that do a particular job

pacemaker (PAYSS-may-kur) a device put in or near the heart to help it beat more regularly

paralysis (puh-RAL-uh-siss) the inability to move or feel a part of one's body

parasites (PA-ruh-sites) organisms that get food and reproduce by living on or in other organisms

severe (suh-VEER) very strong or intense

surgery (SUR-jur-ee) medical treatment that involves fixing or removing diseased or injured parts of the body

symptoms (SIMP-tuhmz) signs of a disease or other physical problems felt by a person

tissue (TISH-oo) a group of similar cells that form a body part or an organ

veterinarian (vet-ur-uh-NER-ee-uhn) a doctor who cares for sick or injured animals

victims (VIK-tuhmz) people who are hurt, killed, or made to suffer

wound (WOOND) an injury in which a person's body is cut and damaged

Index

Bibliography

Altman, Lawrence K. "Lessons of the Kissing Bug's Deadly Gift." *The New York Times* (April 12, 2005).

Davies, David Martin. "How Chagas Disease Is Hidden in Texas." Texas Public Radio Website (November 25, 2015).

Centers for Disease Control and Prevention: www.cdc.gov/parasites/chagas/gen_info/vectors/index.html

Read More

Markovics, Joyce L. *Tiny Invaders! Deadly Microorganisms (Nature's Invaders).* North Mankato, MN: Capstone (2014).

Stewart, Amy. *Wicked Bugs: The Meanest, Deadliest, and Grossest Bugs on Earth.* Chapel Hill, NC: Algonquin (2017).

Learn More Online

To learn more about kissing bugs, visit
www.bearportpublishing.com/BuggedOut

About the Author

Kevin Blake lives in Providence, Rhode Island, with his wife, Melissa, his son, Sam, and his daughter, Ilana. He has written many nonfiction books for kids.